BACK TO CONFESSION

An explanation of Pope John Paul II's Apostolic Exhortation, "Reconciliation and Penance" (*Reconciliatio et Paenitentia*) 2 December 1984 (With a summary of the New Rite and Canon Law)
by
Rev. David Q. Liptak

Foreword
by
Most Rev. John F. Whealon, D.D.
Archbishop of Hartford

IMPRIMATUR
+ Most Rev. John F. Whealon, D.D.
Archbishop of Hartford

The Nihil Obstat and Imprimatur are official declarations that a book or pamphlet is free from doctrinal or moral error. No implications contained therein that those who have granted the Nihil Obstat and Imprimatur agree with the contents, opinions or statements expressed.

27 July 1987

Copyright © 1988 by Liturgical Publications, Inc., 1937 10th Avenue North, Lake Worth, Florida 33461. All rights reserved. No part of this book may be reproduced or transmitted in any form or by any means, electronic or mechanical, including photocopying, recording or by any information storage and retrieval without permission in writing from the Publisher.

ISBN: 0-940169-05-3

To Mary
Mater Salvatoris
This Marian Year
With Appreciation for
Pope John Paul II

Table of Contents

Foreword by Most Rev. John F. Whealon, D.D.,
   Archbishop of Hartford ix
Author's Preface xi
Part I:
Reconciliation and Penance, An Explanation
   Sense of Sin Dulled Today 1
   Sin Always Personal 5
   Sin and Freedom 9
   Mortal and Venial Sin 13
   Two Errors On Sin Today 17
   The Cross and Sin 21
   Dialogue and Conversion 25
   Preaching, Catechesis and Confession 29
   Content of Catechesis 33
   Ministry of Pardon 37
   Penitential Healing 41
   Why Confession Is Needed 45
   Confessional: Blessed Place 49
   Three Forms for Reconciliation 53
Part II:
The New Rite of Penance
   The New Rite of Penance Reviewed (1) 59
   Quick View Of Penance Rites (2) 63
   Anxieties Over New Penance Ritual (3) 67
   Why Individual Absolution Is Norm (4) 71
   Two Now Errors Pertaining To Penance (5) ... 75
   The New Code on Sacrament of Penance (6) ... 79
   Some Closing Thoughts 83

Foreword

As observers of Catholic life testify, the Sacrament of Penance is celebrated much less frequently in Western Europe and North America than a generation ago. Even Catholic parish leaders make use of this sacrament much less frequently than did their parents and ancestors in the faith. The Pope and the bishops are concerned.

Yet at the same time we wonder what ever became of sin in popular consciousness. We wonder whether the younger generation of Catholics see themselves as sinners, in need of their own continuing conversion and God's forgiveness as granted through the Church's priests.

As we do this wondering about others, we need to wonder about ourselves. Are we neglecting this marvelous, helpful sacrament?

That is why I hope Father David Liptak's careful, commendable book on this sacrament — a commentary on the Apostolic Exhortation of Pope John Paul II on "Reconciliation and Penance" — will be received and read with a personal as well as academic approach.

> John F. Whealon, D.D.
> Archbishop of Hartford
> 27 July 1987

Author's Preface

The canonization of Capuchin-Franciscan Father Leopold Mandic, on 16 October 1983, with the sixth general assembly of the world Synod of Bishops *in session*, was an obvious message to the Church today. The Synod's discussions focused on "Reconciliation and Penance in the Church's Mission," and Father Leopold of Castelnuovo was a heroic witness to this theme by means of the confessional.

Yugoslavian by site of birth — Herzeg-Novi (Castelnuovo), Dalmatia, was his birthplace in 1866 — he joined the Capuchins' Venetian branch and made his studies in Italy. Diminutive in stature (four feet, six inches), disadvantaged by a stutter, and not robust in health, he was assigned, after priestly ordination, not to the missions, where he must preach and bear other physical hardships, but to friary service such as assistant cook and official beggar. Later he also served as local superior and a student director. Throughout his early years, however, he devoted himself especially to the ministry of the confessional, and in 1914 this became his principal sacred work, next to offering Mass. He died in Padua, on 30 July 1942.

ST. LEOPOLD became one of the most sought-after confessors of modern times. To his confessional box came penitents from all over Italy: students, military personnel, academicians, peasants, nobles, the rich and poor, religious and priests. And he was regularly invited as a confessor by the bishops of the Venetian Province during their annual retreats.

AMONG Father Leopold's charisms was the power to

read hearts. When the Capuchin house at Padua was leveled by bombs during World War II, the small room wherein he used to hear confessions for 36 years alone remained.

ST. LEOPOLD, Pope John Paul II explained in his homily at the canonization Mass on 16 October, "did not leave us any theological or literary works; he did not attract people with his culture; he did not found any social works. To all those who knew him, he was nothing but a poor friar: small and sickly.

"HIS GREATNESS lay elsewhere: *in immolating himself*, in giving himself, day after day, for the entire span of his priestly life, for fifty-two years, in the silence, in the reserve, in the humility of a confession room . . . Father Leopold was always there, ready and smiling, prudent and modest, the discreet confidant and faithful father of souls, a respectful teacher and an understanding and patient spiritual adviser."

A DESCRIPTION of Father Leopold? A single phrase, the Holy Father said, answers the question; namely, "the confessor." It is in this phrase that this new saint's greatness is found, here — in John Paul's words — "in his fading into the background to give place to the true Shepherd of Souls. He expressed his commitment in this way: 'We hide everything, even what may appear to be a gift of God, so as not to make it an instrument of profit. To God alone be honour and glory! If it were possible, we should pass over the earth like a shadow that leaves no trace.' And to whoever asked him how he could live that way, he would answer, 'It is my life!' "

INCIDENTALLY, one of Father Leopold's special desires was to be a missionary for ecumenism; specifically, to help in the work of reunion between Rome and the separated Eastern Churches. But he knew that God's will was that he should work for unity while dedicating himself to the confessional. "Every soul who seeks my ministry," he would say, "will . . . be my Orient."

CHURCH UNITY, after all, begins with the confessional, with penance and purification. Only when we acknowledge our failings and neglects as prodigal children in the Sacrament of Forgiveness, can we serve a Church purified and purifying toward the unity for which Jesus prayed at the Last Supper (John 10:16).

The material in this book first appeared in substance in the Catholic Transcript (Hartford). I wish to thank all those who helped bring this manuscript to print in a book, especially the Most Rev. John F. Whealon, D.D., Archbishop of Hartford; the Very Rev. Francis J. Lescoe, Ph.D., Rector and President of Holy Apostles Seminary, Cromwell, CT; Attorney Joseph Nucera, J.D.; and the Rev. Joseph LoCigno, S.T.D., Ph.D., of Liturgical Publications.

> Rev. David Q. Liptak
> Solemnity of the Assumption
> of our Blessed Lady, 1987

Sense of Sin Dulled Today

Reconciliatio et Paenitentia ("Reconciliation and Penance"), the 140-page Post-Synodal Apostolic Exhortation issued by Pope John Paul II on 2 December 1984, is a veritable mine of doctrine on sin, conversion and God's merciful forgiveness through Christ's Church.

One key section of the document is that which accents the contemporary world's lack of the sense of sin: Section 18. Down through the centuries, the Holy Father notes, Christians have gained, from the Gospel as it is read in the Church, "a fine sensitivity and an acute perception of the *seeds of death* contained in sin, as well as a sensitivity and an acuteness of perception for identifying them in the thousand guises which sin shows itself." Such is what is commonly referred to as the "sense of sin."

THIS "sense of sin," the Holy Father explains, is rooted in each person's moral conscience and is, as it were, "its thermometer." Linked, obviously, to the "sense of God," because it derives from each one's conscious relationship with God as Creator, Lord and Father, it can no more be totally eradicated than the "sense of God" can be, or any more than conscience can be completely silenced.

THE DULLING of moral conscience (for a host of reasons) is an observable fact of history; it seems to happen not infrequently, and for more or less lengthy periods. "Too many signs indicate that such an eclipse exists in our time," John Paul writes. Moreover, when moral conscience is in eclipse, so is the "sense of sin," which is closely associated with the moral conscience, the quest for truth, and the yearning to make a responsible use of freedom. Too, when moral conscience becomes weak, the "sense of God" is also obscured.

AGREEING with the 1984 Roman Synod of Bishops, John Paul goes on to state that the world today has largely forgotten the "sense of sin" precisely because of a crisis of conscience and a crisis of the "sense of God." Indeed, he recalls the prophetic words of Pope Piux XII: "the sin of the century is the loss of the sense of sin."

WHY HAS this come about? One underlying factor, John Paul states, is "secularism," a humanism totally without God, "completely centered upon the cult of action and production and caught up in the heady enthusiasm of consumerism and pleasure-seeking, unconcerned with the danger of 'losing one's soul.'"

A SECOND factor for the disappearance of sin in contemporary society, the Pope notes, is erroneous application of certain findings in the human sciences. With respect to psychology, for example, concern to avoid "creating feelings of guilt or to place limits on freedom leads to a *refusal ever to admit any shortcoming.*" As regards sociology, there is of course the attempt to blame society for all ills and to declare the individual innocent of them. And in the area of cultural anthropology, environmental and historical conditioning and influences on man are falsely interpreted as excusing him from truly human (i.e., free, responsible, nondetermined) actions.

THIRDLY, a contemporary ethics deriving from a certain historical relativism has obscured the "sense of sin." Thus there are widely accepted theories today which relativize the moral norm, thus denying its absolute and unconditional value (consequently denying that there are intrinsically evil acts).

POPE JOHN PAUL cites as another factor for the decline of the "sense of sin" today erroneous concepts of sin as propagated in the mass media, in the formation of youths and even in education — concepts such as the identification of sin with merely a morbid feeling of guilt or with the mere transgression of legal norms or precepts.

THE HOLY FATHER readily admits that part of the problem can be found within certain trends served by some who claim to serve the Church: deficiencies in the practice of sacramental Penance (from "routine ritualism" to an overemphasis on the social nature of sin); inadequacies or errors in catechesis, theological teaching, spiritual direction and preaching, etc.

THE GRAVE spiritual crisis looming over men today must be first addressed by the restoration of a "sense of sin," the Holy Father argues. How? Principally, he replies, "by sound catechetics, illuminated by the biblical theology of the Covenant, by an attentive listening and trustful openness to the Magisterium of the Church, which never ceases to enlighten consciences, and by an ever more careful practice of the Sacrament of Penance."

Sin Always Personal

One of the great moral confusions of our times is failure to grasp the concept of *personal* sin in the context of so-called "social sin." As a result many persons today are quick to blame their own wrongdoing on society (e.g., "No one's to blame; society is to blame"), thus claiming themselves excused from guilt. Pope John Paul II discusses this subject in Section 16 of *Reconciliatio et Paenitentia*.

SIN, the Holy Father emphasizes, is *always a personal act*. Sin is an act of freedom, a choice, by an individual person, and not properly of a group of persons. That the individual sinner can be conditioned or swayed by societal factors goes without saying. That, moreover, he or she may be subjected to tendencies, defects and habits that may in not a few cases attenuate, to a greater or lesser degree, his or her freedom and, hence, his or her responsibility and guilt, is also evident. Nonetheless, John Paul reasserts, it is "a truth of faith, also confirmed by our experience and reason, that the human person is free."

PERSONAL FREEDOM, therefore, cannot be disregarded in order to place the blame for the individual's sins on structures, systems or other people. On the contrary, "there is nothing so personal and untransferable in each individual as merit for virtue or responsibility for sin."

WHAT THEN is "social sin"? Here the Holy Father offers three senses.

FIRST, he states, "social sin" constitutes recognition

that "by virtue of a human solidarity which is as mysterious and intangible as it is real and concrete, each individual's sin in some way affects others." Using an expression coined by the French writer Elisabeth Leseur, to wit, "every soul that rises above itself, raises up the world," John Paul says that the opposite is also true; namely, "every soul that lowers itself through sin drags down with itself the Church, and, in some way, the whole world." To the "law of ascent," the "law of descent" corresponds. There is no sin, not even the most secret, that exclusively concerns the individual sinner; every sin has repercussions on the entire ecclesial body, and hence is "social."

ANOTHER context of "social sin" is that of interpersonal relationships, whether individuals alone, or individuals and the community, are involved. Therefore "social" is every sin — in John Paul's words — "against the rights of the human person, beginning with the right to life and including the life of the unborn, or against a person's physical integrity. Likewise *social* is every sin against others' freedom . . . [and] against the dignity and honor of one's neighbor. Also *social* is every sin against the common good . . ."

THIRDLY, John Paul explains, "social sin" refers to the relationships between the various human communities. The context here would include, for example, "the class struggle" — whoever the person who leads or tries to justify it. Likewise, he adds, "obstinate confrontation between blocs of nations, between one nation and another, between different groups within the same nation." The sense of "social sin" here (because realities and situations reach vast proportions as social phenomena and almost always become anonymous, just as their causes are not always identifiable) obviously has an analogical sense. But, John Paul warns, "to speak even analogically of *social sins* must not cause us to underestimate the responsibility of the *individuals* involved. It is meant to be an appeal to the consciences of all . . . in order to change . . . disastrous conditions and intolerable situations." (Italics added)

THE PROBLEM of confusion today, John Paul concludes, is complex. First, "social sin" cannot be contrasted from "personal sin" in the error that personal guilt can be watered down. On the contrary, personal sin is the reality. Further, when we validly speak of "social sin" — with respect to, say, situations of sin or the collective action of social groups or nations — we mean "the result of the accumulation of concentration of many personal sins . . . of those who cause or support evil or who exploit it; of those who are in a position to avoid, eliminate or at least limit certain social evils but who fail to do so, out of laziness, fear or the conspiracy of silence, through secret complicity or indifference; of those who take refuge in the supposed impossibility of changing the world . . ."

AT THE HEART of every sinful *situation*, the Holy Father declares — injustice, hunger, poverty — *are always to be found sinful people.*

Sin and Freedom

Sin, Pope John Paul II explains in his magnificent Apostolic Exhortation *Reconciliatio et Paenitentia*, is a product of man's freedom. However, "deep within its human reality there are factors at work which place it beyond the merely human, in the border area where man's conscience, will and sensitivity are in contact with the dark forces which, according to St. Paul, are active in the world almost to the point of ruling it." (Romans 7:7-25; Ephesians 2:2; 6:12)

One biblical story that is especially instructive as regards an understanding of sin is that of the Tower of Babel. (Genesis 11:1-9) The people of Babel tried to found a city, organize themselves into a society and achieve strength *without God*, if not precisely *against God*. Like our first parents in the Garden of Eden, they tried to achieve a worldly goal by excluding God, at least with the attitude that God has no relevance in the sphere of man's joint ventures.

"*Exclusion of God, rupture with God, disobedience to God:* throughout the history of mankind this has been, and is, in various forms, *sin*," the Holy Father asserts. "It can go as far as a very *denial* of God and his existence: this is the phenomenon called *atheism*.

"IT IS the disobedience of a person who, by a free act, does not acknowledge God's sovereignty over his or her life, at least at that particular moment in which he or she transgresses God's law." (Sec. 14)

WHY DID the Tower of Babel fail? It failed, John Paul answers, because the people "had set up as a sign and guarantee of the unity they desired a work of their hands alone, and had forgotten the action of the Lord. They had attended only to the horizontal dimension of work and social life, forgetting the vertical dimension by which they would have been rooted in God, their Creator and Lord, and would have been directed toward him as the ultimate goal of their progress." (Sec. 13)

MAN'S BREAK from God through sin also leads tragically to divisions between brothers and sisters.

THIS is clear, the Holy Father notes, from a reading of the consequences of Adam's sin. The first man and woman pointed accusingly at each other — separation. Later, one son hated his brother and took his life.

IN THE STORY of Babel, the human family as a whole was shattered by sin.

HERE John Paul presents a theological analysis of sin and its consequences. It must be cited in full:

"NO ONE wishing to investigate the mystery of sin can ignore this link between cause and effect. As a rupture with God, sin is an act of disobedience by a creature who rejects, at least implicitly, the very one from whom he came and who sustains him in life. It is therefore a suicidal act. Since by sinning man refuses to submit to God, his internal balance is also destroyed and it is precisely within himself that contradictions and conflicts arise. Wounded in this way, man almost inevitably causes damage to the fabric of his relationship with others and with the created world. This is an objective reality, verified in so many ways in the human psyche and in the spiritual life, as well as in society, where it is easy to see the signs and effects of internal disorder.

"THE MYSTERY of sin is composed of this twofold wound which the sinner opens in himself and in his relationship with his neighbor. Therefore one can speak of *personal* and *social* sin: from one point of view, every sin is *personal*; from another point of view every sin is *social*, in so far as and because it also has social repercussions."

Mortal and Venial Sin

Having reaffirmed the reality of sin as a *personal* act which entails *personal* guilt, Pope John Paul II moves on, in his Apostolic Constitution *Reconciliatio et Paenitentia*, to the distinction between mortal and venial sin.

The distinction cannot be overlooked.

Already, in the Old Testament Scriptures, certain sins, committed deliberately, were deemed grave violations of God's word: idolatry, for example. See Numbers 15:30, Leviticus 18:26-30, Exodus 21:7. Contrasted from such sins were other faults, of lesser significance, though sins nonetheless. See Leviticus 4:2 sqq., Numbers 15:22-29.

IN NEW TESTAMENT Revelation, the distinction is subjected to greater light. See Matthew 5:28, 6:23, 12:31 sqq., 15:19; also Mark 3:28-20; also Romans 1:29-31, 13:13; also James 4.

IN THE FIRST Letter of John (5:16 sqq.), the Holy Father observes, we read of a sin *which leads to death* (in the original Greek, *pros thanaton*) as opposed to a sin which *does not lead to death* (*me pros thanaton*). The context is obviously *spiritual death.* The sacred writer's intention, the Pope notes, is (1) "to emphasize the incalculable seriousness of what constitutes the very essence of sin, namely, the rejection of God," and also (2) "to underline the certainty that comes to the Christian from the fact of having been 'born of God' through the coming of the Son: the Christian possesses a power that preserves him from falling into sin; God protects him and 'the evil one does not touch him.' If he should sin through weakness or ignorance, he has confidence in being forgiven, also because he is supported by the joint prayer of the community."

FURTHER, in Matthew's Gospel, Jesus speaks of a sin — a "blasphemy against the Holy Spirit" which "will not be forgiven," since it constitutes an obstinate refusal to be converted to the love of God, the Father of Mercies. This text especially confirms the existence of sins which can effect eternal death.

PONDERING biblical texts which distinguish grave sins from others, the Church Fathers, theologians, spiritual teachers and pastors have from the beginning distinguished between, on the one hand, mortal or serious sins, and, on the other hand, venial or light sins. St. Augustine was one who led the way in explaining this distinction, and St. Thomas Aquinas formulated it in precise terminology.

"WITH the whole Tradition of Church," John Paul writes, "we call *mortal sin* the act by which man freely and consciously rejects God, his law, the covenant of love that God offers, preferring to turn in on himself or to some created and finite reality, something contrary to the divine will . . . This can occur in a direct and formal way, in the sins of idolatry, apostasy and atheism; or in an equivalent way, as in every act of disobedience to God's commandments in a grave matter. Man perceives that this disobedience to God destroys the bond that unites him with his life-principle; it is a *mortal sin*, that is, an act which gravely offends God and ends in turning against man himself with a dark and powerful force of destruction." (Sec. 17)

THE SYNOD of 1984, Pope John Paul reminds, not

only reaffirmed the doctrine of the Council of Trent concerning the existence and nature of mortal and venial sin, but it also recalled "that *mortal sin* is sin whose object is grave matter and which is also committed with full knowledge and deliberate consent."

ACCORDING to St. Thomas and other Doctors, the Pope goes on, *mortal* sin is the sin which, if unforgiven, leads to eternal punishment; whereas *venial* sin is the sin that merits merely temporal punishment (that is, a partial punishment which can be expiated on earth or in Purgatory).

AQUINAS taught that man, in order to live spiritually, must remain in communion with the supreme principle of life; namely, God, because God is the ultimate goal of man's being and acting. But sin constitutes a disorder opted for by man against this life-principle. And when, "through sin, the soul commits a disorder that reaches the point of turning away from its ultimate end — God — to which it is bound by charity, then the sin is mortal sin; on the other hand, whenever the disorder does not reach the point of a turning away from God, the sin is venial." (*Summa Theologiae*, I-II, q. 72, a. 5; translation as cited by John Paul II).

Two Errors On Sin Today

In his *Reconciliatio et Paenitentia*, his post-Synodal Apostolic Exhortation, Pope John Paul II takes time to single out two contemporary errors in moral theology. One has to do with attempts to challenge the traditional doctrine of objective morality. The other pertains to fallacies regarding the so-called "fundamental option."

As for the first, the constant teaching of the Church is reaffirmed: some sins are intrinsically *grave* and *mortal* by reason of their matter. This is to say that — in the Holy Father's own words — "there exist acts which, *per se* and in themselves, independently of circumstances, are always seriously wrong by reason of their object." (Sec. 17)

THIS CLEAR and perennial teaching, John Paul explains, is founded on the Decalogue (the Ten Commandments), "and assimilated into the *kerygma* of the Apostles . . ." It belongs to the Church's earliest teaching, and has been repeatedly reaffirmed by the Church down through the centuries, up to the current hour. Besides, the Pope adds, "it is exactly verified in the experience of the men and women of all times . . ." (Ibid.)

ONE PROBLEM today in moral theology is a reluctance to admit the intrinsic evil of certain acts — direct abortion, for instance. Consequentialist and extreme proportionalist theories evaluating morality would reject the reality of objective morality (possibly with some exceptions, depending on the particular theory), and seek (wrongly, of course) to discover the morality of an action solely in its consequences. Certain of these theories even suggest a distinction between moral evil and what is described as "premoral" (or "ontic") evil. Some cruder theories, also rejecting the possibility of intrinsically evil actions, would assess morality in terms of each and every "situation" or "context."

AGAINST such theories, John Paul and the 1984 Roman Synod unequivocally reassert the traditional doctrine that some sins are *intrinsically* grave and mortal by virtue of their matter.

THE SECOND contemporary erroneous theory about sin singled out by John Paul in his Apostolic Exhortation concerns the concept of "fundamental option," a widely discussed, but, in my judgment, little understood theologism.

HERE it would be best to follow Pope John Paul's words precisely:

"LIKEWISE, care will have to be taken not to reduce mortal sin to an act of *'fundamental option'* — as is commonly said today — against God, intending thereby an explicit and formal contempt for God or neighbor. For mortal sin exists also when a person knowingly and willingly, for whatever reason, chooses something gravely disordered. In fact, such a choice already includes contempt for the divine law, a rejection of God's love for humanity and the whole of creation: the person turns away from God and loses charity. Thus the fundamental orientation can be radically changed by individual acts. Clearly there can occur situations which are very complex and obscure from a psychological viewpoint, and which have an influence on the sinner's subjective culpability. But from a consideration of the psychological sphere one cannot proceed to the construction of a theological category, which is what the 'fundamental option' precisely is, understanding it in such a way that it objectively changes or casts doubt upon the traditional concept of mortal sin.

"WHILE every sincere and prudent attempt to clarify the psychological and theological mystery of sin is to be valued, the Church nevertheless has a duty to remind all scholars in this field of the need to be faithful to the word of God that teaches us also about sin. She likewise has to remind them of the risk of contributing to a further weakening of the sense of sin in the modern world."

Reconciliatio et Paenitentia is a document that brightly mirrors John Paul II's expertise as a moral theologian. In it, we hear not only the Holy Father, the Rock of Orthodoxy, but also the Holy Father, a highly attuned, extremely learned ethician — The Ethician of Lublin, as he was known long before ascending to Peter's chair.

The Cross and Sin

Since sin is a *personal* act by which a man or woman freely turns from God, the only way that the sinner can liberate himself or herself from sin and its results is by freely repudiating his or her evil act and turning to God for forgiveness. Yet God, our faith tells us, is both willing and ready to forgive. Indeed, God *is the one who makes the first move*, as it were, by inviting the sinner to return.

Pope John Paul II brings this theology out boldly in the early sections of his Apostolic Exhortation *Reconciliatio et Paenitentia.*

RECONCILIATION of the sinner is primarily a *gift of God.* The initiative is on God's part! And this initiative is concretized in the mystery of Christ the Redeemer, the Reconciler and Liberator of human beings from sin in all its forms. This is a theme at the center of St. Paul's Christology. In Christ, Paul writes, the Father has reconciled all creatures to himself; he is our peace and our reconciliation. (See Colossians 1:20-22; Romans 5:10 sqq.; Second Corinthians 5:18, 10; Ephesians 2:14.)

ST. JOHN, in his Gospel, speaks of reconciliation in another manner; namely, that of Jesus' going to the Cross of Calvary "to gather into one the children of God who are scattered abroad." (11:52) *Not only does sin separate man from God, but it also shatters the human community.* This aspect of sin is also accented in Luke's story of the Prodigal Son, specifically in the reference to the Prodigal's elder brother who both rebukes his brother and refuses to celebrate his homecoming.

"MAN — every human being — is also this elder

brother," John Paul explains. Selfishness makes him jealous, hardens his heart, blinds him, and shuts him off from other people and from God. The loving kindness and mercy of the father irritate and engage him; for him the happiness of the brother who has been found again has a bitter taste. From this point of view he too needs to be converted in order to be reconciled." (Sec. 6)

THE CROSS of Jesus is, John Paul states, the answer to this "horizontal" shattering of mankind as well as the "vertical." Sin, which separates man from God and, by virtue of this, shatters human community, was conquered by the Cross.

WRITES John Paul:

"IT IS precisely before the sad spectacle of the divisions and difficulties in the way of reconciliation *between people* that I invite all to look to the *mysterium Crucis* as the loftiest drama in which Christ perceives and suffers to the greatest possible extent the tragedy of the division of man from God, so that he cries out in the words of the Psalmist: 'My God, my God, why have you forsaken me?' and at the same time accomplishes our reconciliation. With our eyes fixed on the mystery of Golgotha we should be reminded always of that *'vertical' dimension* of division and reconciliation concerning the relationship between man and God, a dimension which in the eyes of faith always prevails over the *'horizontal' dimension*, that is to say, over the reality of division between people and the need for reconciliation between them. For we know that reconciliation between people is and can only be the fruit of the redemptive act of Christ, who died and rose again to conquer the kingdom of sin, to reestablish the covenant with God and thus break down the dividing wall which sin had raised up between people." (Sec. 7)

RECONCILIATION — everything that the Son of God Incarnate did and taught for the reconciliation of the world — is now experienced in Christ's Church. To the Apostles upon whom he founded his Church, Christ conferred the *ministry of reconciliation*, a ministry they — those ordained to presbyteral service — carry out today *in persona Christi* ["in the person of Christ"].

TO THE CHURCH as a whole, moreover, to the whole community of believers, Christ entrusted, in various other ways, the *message of reconciliation.*

Dialogue and Conversion

To the Church, Pope John Paul II stresses in his Apostolic Exhortation *Reconciliatio et Paenitentia*, Christ has entrusted the pastoral ministry of penance and reconciliation. How does the Church fulfill this trust? First, by preaching and catechesis. Secondly, by the sacraments, and in a special way, the Sacrament of Penance. Both these means are best comprehended today according to "the method of dialogue."

As John Paul put it:

"PASTORAL DIALOGUE aimed at reconciliation continues to be today a fundamental task of the Church in different spheres and at different levels." (Sec. 25)

THUS, there is *ecumenical dialogue.* The Catholic Church, "actively engaged in seeking her own internal communion," John Paul explains, "can address an appeal for reconciliation to the other Churches with which there does not exist full communion, as well as to other religions and even to all those who are seeking God with a sincere heart . . ." (Ibid.)

AND: "To the extent to which the Church is capable of generating active harmony — unity in variety — within herself, and of offering herself as a witness to and humble servant of reconciliation with the other Churches and ecclesial communities and the other religions, she becomes, in the expressive definition of Saint Augustine, a *reconciled world . . . Then she will be able to be a sign of reconciliation in the world and for the world."* (Ibid.)

THE CHURCH'S dialogue toward reconciliation is

admittedly complex and delicate. John Paul speaks of the work of the Holy See in the area of peace and justice, of humanitarian goals in general, a work inspired by the conviction that as "in war two parties rise against one another," so "in the question of peace there are also necessarily two parties which must know how to commit themselves . . ." (Ibid.)

THE CHURCH also engages in dialogue for reconciliation through its bishops, either individually or united in their national conferences, with the collaboration of their priests and laity. Here the Pope's words are especially powerful:

"THEY TRULY fulfill their task when they promote this indispensable dialogue and proclaim the human and Christian need for reconciliation and peace. In communion with their Pastors, the laity who have as 'their own field of evangelizing activity . . . the vast and complicated world of politics, society . . . economics . . . (and) international life', are called upon to engage directly in dialogue or to work for dialogue aimed at reconciliation. Through them too the Church carries out her reconciling activity. Thus the fundamental presupposition and secure basis for any lasting renewal of society and for peace between nations lies in the regeneration of hearts through conversion and penance.

"IT SHOULD be repeated that, on the part of the Church and her members, dialogue, whatever form it takes (and these forms can be and are very diverse, since the very concept of dialogue has an analogical value), can never begin from an attitude of indifference to the truth. On the contrary, it must begin from a presentation of the truth, offered in a calm way, with respect for the intelligence and consciences of others. The dialogue of reconciliation can never replace or attenuate the proclamation of the truth of the Gospel, the precise goal of which is conversion from sin and communion with Christ and the Church. It must be at the services of the transmission and realization of that truth through the means left by Christ to the Church for the pastoral activity of reconciliation, namely catechesis and penance."

ALL OF THIS — this mode of dialogue — helps lead people to conversion and repentance, along the path of renewal of their own lives. Authentic dialogue is oriented, above all else, at the revival or rebirth of individuals, through interior conversion and repentance, but always with profound respect for consciences and with patience "at the step-by-step pace indispensable for modern conditions."

THE MEANS toward penance and reconciliation, as I noted above, are preaching and catechesis, and the sacraments.

Preaching, Catechesis and Confession

Two principal means by which the Church in dialogue promotes its pastoral ministry of reconciliation and penance are (1) preaching and catechesis, and (2) the Sacrament of Penance. This, Pope John Paul II explains in Section 26, of his masterly post-Synodal Apostolic Exhortation, *Reconciliatio et Paenitentia*.

First, he discusses catechesis.

From the Church's pastors — the bishops and priests, in the first place — the Church expects adequate teaching *on reconciliation*. Such a catechesis, the Holy Father reminds, "must be founded on the teaching of the Bible, especially the New Testament, on the need to rebuild the covenant with God in Christ the Redeemer and Reconciler."

MOREOVER, this teaching, "in the light of this new communion and friendship" (the new Covenant), must be structured on the doctrine concerning "the need to be reconciled with one's brethren, even if this means interrupting the offering of the sacrifice." (Matthew 5:23 sqq.)

THE CHURCH'S pastors are also likewise obliged to offer the faithful an adequate catechesis *on penance*. Here, too, the Bible as read within the Church must be the base for the message provided. This message stresses the need for conversion, the Greek term for which is *metanoia*; literally, to permit the spirit to be overturned to make it turn Godward. No reconciliation is possible unless conversion — an attitude of conversion — precedes. Catechesis, the Holy Father insists, should explain all this with concepts and words or phrases adapted to people's various ages, and socio-cultural, moral backgrounds.

THAT *penance entails repentance* should also be taught, John Paul adds. Here he recalls Luke 17:3 sqq., the passage warning us to forgive our repentant brothers or sisters again and again. "A good catechesis," the Pope writes, "will show how repentance, just like conversion, is far from being a superficial feeling but a real overturning of the soul."

ALSO ESSENTIAL in penance, the Holy Father states, is *doing penance* — i.e., "the movement whereby the preceding attitudes of conversion and repentance are manifested externally." *To do penance* means in the first place "to re-establish the balance and harmony broken by sin, to change direction even at the cost of sacrifice."

A SOLID catechesis on penance is especially important today because of confusion in our secular environment. Dominant views in psychology and social behavior are currently at odds with the biblical norms of penance and reconciliation. In John Paul's words:

"CONTEMPORARY man seems to find it harder than ever to recognize his own mistakes and to decide to retrace his steps and begin again after changing course. He seems very reluctant to say 'I repent' or 'I am sorry.' He seems to refuse instinctively, and often irresistibly, anything that is penance in the sense of a sacrifice accepted and carried out for the correction of sin. In this regard I would like to emphasize that *the Church's penitential discipline*, even though it has been mitigated for some time, cannot be abandoned without grave harm to the interior life of individual Christians and of the ecclesial community, and also to their capacity for missionary influence. It is not uncommon for non-Christians to be surprised at the negligible witness of true penance on the part of Christ's followers. It is clear, however, that Christian penance will only be authentic if it is inspired by love and not by mere fear; if it consists in a serious effort to crucify the 'old man' so that the 'new' can be born by the power of Christ; if it takes as its model Christ, who though he was innocent chose the path of poverty, patience, austerity, and, one can say, the penitential life."

CATECHESIS today must also include *authentic doctrine on conscience and its formation.* This too, is a current problem, because of our secular climate. John Paul explains:

"VALUABLE guidelines for a wise catechesis on conscience can be found both in the Doctors of the Church and in the theology of the Second Vatican Council, and especially in the documents on the Church in the Modern World and on religious liberty. Along these same lines, Pope Paul VI often reminded us of the nature and role of conscience in our life. I myself, following his footsteps, miss no opportunity to throw light on this most lofty element of man's greatness and dignity, this 'sort of *moral sense* which leads us to discern what is *good* and what is *evil* . . . like an inner eye, a visual capacity of the spirit, able to guide our steps along the path of good.' And I have reiterated the need to form one's own conscience, lest it become 'a force which is destructive of the true humanity of the person, rather than that holy place where God reveals to him his true good.'"

Content of Catechesis

As he proximately approaches the key point of the Sacrament of Penance in his post-Synodal Apostolic Exhortation *Reconciliatio et Paenitentia*, Pope John Paul II accents the crucial importance of adequate preaching and catechesis. (Section 26) He then details several areas on which this preaching or catechesis should focus.

First, of course, pastors and their associates or helpers must teach about *conscience and its formation.* He reminds that a treasure of authentic source material is available for this: the Church's pronouncements, especially Vatican Council II (e.g., The Church in the Modern World) and the statements of the Doctors of the Church. He also singles out Pope Paul VI, who spoke often about the nature and role of conscience. John Paul describes conscience as that "sort of *moral sense* which leads us to discern what is *good* and what is *evil* . . . Like an inner eye, a visual capacity of the spirit, able to guide our steps along the path of good." Conscience, therefore is *not a feeling.* And John Paul stresses the need to *form one's conscience*, lest it become a force destructive of the true humanity of the person.

SECONDLY, the Pope insists, the *sense of sin* must be taught — especially since it has been weakened in our world.

THIRDLY, John Paul writes, catechesis must stress the reality of *temptation and temptations.* Temptations do not constitute sins, he reminds. But prayer not to succumb to temptation is needed. Here he also speaks about a subject which, like sin, the modern world tries to ignore; namely, the occasion of sin.

CATECHESIS is also expected with regard to *fasting*, by forms old and new. Fasting of course steels us against temptation to sin. And it is a sign of union with Christ and solidarity with the suffering.

Almsgiving too should be taught about. It serves to render charity a practical thing.

TOO, there should be catechesis on the *intimate connection* which links the "overcoming of divisions in the world with perfect communion with God and among people, which is the eschatological purpose of the Church."

NEXT, there is the need for catechesis on the *concrete circumstances* in which reconciliation has to be secured — in the family, in the civil sphere, in social structures, particularly on the four basic fragmentations: reconciliation of man (1) with God, (2) with self, (3) with one's brothers and sisters and (4) with the whole of creation.

NOR CAN catechesis omit instruction on the *four last things of man:* (1) death, (2) judgment, universal and particular, (3) hell and (4) heaven. In the Holy Father's words:

"IN A CULTURE which tends to imprison man in the earthly life at which he is more or less successful, the pastors of the Church are asked to provide a catechesis which will reveal and illustrate with the certainties of faith what comes after the present life: beyond the mysterious gates of death, an eternity of joy in communion with God or the punishment of separation from him. Only in this eschatological vision can one realize the exact nature of sin and feel decisively moved to penance and reconciliation."

HOW is this catechesis to be given? Here John Paul relies largely on his experiential grasp of the problem:

"PASTORS who are zealous and creative never lack opportunities for imparting this broad and varied catechesis, taking into account the different degrees of education and religious formation of those to whom they speak. Such opportunities are often given by the biblical readings and the rites of the Mass and the Sacraments, as also by the circumstances of their celebration. For the same purpose many initiatives can be taken such as sermons, lectures, discussions, meetings, courses of religious education, etc., as happens in many places. Here I wish to point out in particular the importance and effectiveness of the old-style *popular missions* for the purposes of such catechesis. If adapted to the peculiar needs of the present time, such missions can be, today as yesterday, a useful instrument of religious education also regarding penance and reconciliation."

FINALLY, the Holy Father reminds that an adequate catechesis for reconciliation and penance must include reference to *the Church's social teachings.*

Ministry of Pardon

After explaining the *message* of penance and reconciliation in his monumental Apostolic Constitution, *Reconciliatio et Paenitentia*, Pope John Paul II writes about the *ministry* of penance and reconciliation.

The ministry is defined primarily in the sacraments, especially in the one which "has often been called the Sacrament of *Confession* because of the accusation of sins that takes place in it" but which "can more appropriately be considered . . . the *Sacrament of Penance*, as it is in fact called."

NOTING that the Synod of Bishops, during its deliberations, had often stated that the Sacrament of Penance is in crisis, John Paul emphasizes that it is good to renew and reaffirm our faith in this *great Sacrament*.

THERE IS no question, the Holy Father maintains, that through the Sacrament of Penance Christ has empowered mere men — his ordained priests — to take away sins in his name:

"JUST as at the altar where he celebrates the Eucharist, and just as in each one of the Sacraments, so the priest, as the minister of Penance, acts *in persona Christi*. The Christ whom he makes present and who accomplishes the mystery of the forgiveness of sins is the Christ who appears as the *brother of man* . . . , the merciful High Priest, faithful and compassionate, . . . the Shepherd intent on finding the lost sheep . . . the Physician who heals and comforts . . . the Judge of the living and the dead . . . who judges according to the truth . . ." (Sec. 29)

SPEAKING from his own pastoral experience, no doubt, the Holy Father describes the priest's ministry as confessor as "the most difficult and sensitive, the most exhausting and demanding," but at the same time "one of the most beautiful and consoling."

FOR THIS ministry, the Pope goes on, the confessor is absolutely in need of certain human qualities: prudence, discretion, discernment and "a firmness tempered by gentleness and kindness."

FURTHERMORE, priests need special training, a preparation not fragmentary but complete and harmonious, first in crucial theological areas, then in pedagogy and psychology, then in the methodology of dialogue, and "above all in a living and communicable knowledge of the word of God." Fundamentally, of course, the confessor must be a person whose spiritual life is genuine and intense.

HERE the Holy Father insists that the priest must be trained "for the ministry of sacramental Penance from his years in the seminary," not only through formal studies (dogmatic, moral, spiritual and pastoral theology), but also through a knowledge of the human sciences, training in dialogue, and "especially on how to deal with people in the pastoral context." And every priest must continually update his art and skills as a confessor. "What a wealth of grace, true life and spiritual radiation would be poured out on the Church," he writes, "if every priest were careful never to miss, through negligence or various excuses, the appointment with the faithful in the confessional, and if he were even more careful never to go to it unprepared or lacking the necessary human qualities and spiritual and pastoral preparation!"

AS EXAMPLES of what the ministry of Penance can effect in the world, John Paul cites several priests synonymous with the role of confessor: St. John Nepomucene (who died a martyr to the seal of confession); St. John Vianney (who changed his village of Ars largely through his devotion to the Sacrament of Reconciliation); St. Joseph Cafasso and St. Leopold of Castelnuovo (whom John Paul canonized during the Synod on Penance and Reconciliation). And he goes on "to pay homage" to the countless many "holy and almost always anonymous confessors to whom is owed the salvation of so many souls who have been helped by them in conversion, in the struggle against sin and temptation, in spiritual progress and, in a word, in achieving holiness."

SUCH CONFESSORS, those of us who profess the Faith, have known, many of us from our childhood. Indeed, it is an unwritten principle universally accepted among Catholics that the measure of a priest is not only his devotion and fidelity to the Eucharist and to preaching the word, but also his commitment and love for the ministry as father confessor. This has been especially true during the confusion about the Sacrament of Penance that was spawned by inadequate or false theologies in the aftermath of Vatican II.

Penitential Healing

From the Church's beginning, Pope John Paul II recalls in his *Reconciliatio et Paenitentia*, it has both recognized and employed many varying forms of penance. The penitential act in Mass is one example; fasting, another; pilgrimage, a third. But none of these compares in significance or divine efficacy with the Sacrament of Penance. It is *the* special means instituted by Christ for the forgiveness of sins committed after baptism.

The practice of sacramental penance, the Holy Father explains, "has undergone a long process of development, as is attested to by the most ancient sacramentaries, the documents of councils and Episcopal Synods, the preaching of the Fathers, and the teaching of the Doctors of the Church." But, he adds, with respect to the substance of the Sacrament, "there has always remained firm and unchanged in the consciousness of the Church *the certainty* that, by the will of Christ, forgiveness is offered to each individual by means of sacramental absolution given by the ministers of Penance."

HERE John Paul sets forth a series of basic convictions regarding the Sacrament of Penance — "convictions of faith" he calls them.

FIRST, he writes, for a Christian, the Sacrament of Penance *is the ordinary way of obtaining forgiveness and the remission of serious sins committed after baptism.*

THUS, whereas the Savior and his salvific action "are not so bound to a sacramental sign as to be unable in any period or area of history of salvation to work outside the sacraments," the same Savior nonetheless "desired and provided that the simple and precious Sacraments of faith would ordinarily be the effective means through which his redemptive power passes and operates."

HENCE, it would be "foolish, as well as presumptuous" arbitrarily to wish to disregard the means of grace and salvation which the Savior has provided, and, in a specific instance, "to claim to receive forgiveness while doing without the Sacrament of Penance."

THE LITURGICAL renewal of the Rite of Penance, dating from Vatican II, was meant to emphasize the above stated doctrine, not detract from it. The new Rite, John Paul states, "was and is meant to stir up in each one of us a *new impulse* toward the renewal of our interior attitude; toward a deeper understanding of the nature of the Sacrament of Penance; toward a reception of the Sacrament which is more filled with faith, not anxious but trusting; toward a more frequent celebration of the sacrament which is seen to be completely filled with the Lord's merciful love."

A SECOND "conviction of faith" regarding Penance cited by John Paul is that it involves both a *judicial action* and a *healing of a medicinal character.*

WHILE PENANCE is judicial, the tribunal for it is one of mercy rather than one of "strict and rigorous justice." Indeed, the tribunal of Penance is comparable to human tribunals only by analogy; "namely insofar as sinners reveal their sins and their condition as creatures subject to sin; accept the punishment . . . which the confessor imposes on them; and receive absolution from him."

THE CHARACTER of judgment pertaining to the

Sacrament of Penance is, however, one of *healing*. Long ago St. Augustine, referring to his work as father confessor, said, "I wish to heal, not accuse."

THE NEW RITE of Penance accents this healing aspect, to which contemporary man is perhaps especially sensitive, since he views sin not only in terms of error, but even moreso in terms of weakness and human frailty.

WHETHER Penance is perceived as a tribunal of mercy or a place of healing, the Holy Father concludes, "the Sacrament requires a knowledge of the sinner's heart, in order to be able to judge and absolve, to care and heal. Precisely for this reason the Sacrament involves, on the part of the penitent, a sincere and complete confession of sins."

HENCE confession is not simply an ascetical exercise, meant to aid humility, say, or to serve mortification. Rather, confession "*is inherent* in the very nature of the Sacrament."

Why Confession Is Needed

After Pope John Paul II, in his *Reconciliatio et Paenitentia*, stresses sacramental Penance as (1) the ordinary means instituted by Christ for forgiveness of serious postbaptismal sins and (2) a means of mercy, he proceeds to a third "conviction of faith"; namely, the so-called "parts" which constitute the sacramental sign of forgiveness and reconciliation. (Sec. 31)

Among these "parts" are, first of all the "acts of the penitent," traditionally described by the Church as *contrition, confession* and *satisfaction*. The fourth "part" is the ministry of the priest; specifically, *absolution*.

THE ACTS of the penitent must, of course, reflect "rectitude and clarity of . . . conscience." This is an "indispensable condition" for Penance. Hence, persons "cannot come to true and genuine repentance until they realize that sin is contrary to the ethical norm written in their inmost being; . . . until they admit that they have had a personal and responsible experience of this contrast; until they say not only that 'sin exists' but also 'I have sinned'; until they admit that sin has introduced a division into their consciences, which then pervades their whole being and separates them from God and from their brothers and sisters."

THUS, an *examination of conscience* is requisite prior to sacramental confession. This must never take the form, John Paul writes, "of anxious psychological introspection" but rather of "a sincere and calm comparison with the interior moral law, with the evangelical norms proposed by the Church, with Jesus Christ himself who is our Teacher and Model of life, and with the heavenly Father, who calls us to goodness and perfection." (Ibid.)

AN ESSENTIAL act of penance, insofar as the penitent is concerned, is of course *contrition.* The Holy Father reasserts this, and describes it; namely, "a clear and decisive rejection of the sin committed, together with a resolution not to commit it again . . . out of the love which one has for God and which is reborn with repentance."

ONE SPECIFIC aspect of contrition that the Holy Father emphasizes here is that contrition and conversion, while making profound demands in terms of mortification for a radical change of life, also and more significantly constitute a "drawing near to the holiness of God, a rediscovery of one's true identity . . . upset and distributed by . . . sin, a liberation in the very depth of self, and thus a regaining of lost joy, the joy of being saved, . . . which the majority of people in our time are no longer capable of experiencing."

THIS MAKES it easier to understand the need for confession in the Sacrament of Penance, an act so identifiable with the Sacrament that for centuries its "usual name . . . has been and still is . . . *Confession.*"

WHY IS the confession of sins required? The Holy Father recalls the traditional reasons, perennially relevant. First, confession is needed so that the sinner might be known by the priest who in the sacrament acts in the role of judge, who must evaluate both the seriousness of the sins and the repentance of the sinner. Secondly, since the priest serves also as healer, he must know the condition of the penitent's spiritual illness.

A THIRD reason pertains to the sign-value of the sacrament. Individual confession, John Paul explains, implies "a sign of the meeting of the sinner with the mediation of the Church in the person of the minister; a sign of the person's revealing of self as a sinner in the sight of God and the Church, of facing his own sinful condition in the eyes of God."

HENCE, the Pope continues, "confession of sins . . . cannot be reduced to an attempt at psychological liberation, even though it corresponds to that legitimate and natural need, inherent in the human heart, to open oneself to another." Rather, "it is a liturgical act, solemn in its dramatic gesture, yet humble and sober in the grandeur of its meaning. It is the act of the Prodigal Son who returns to the Father and is welcomed by him with the kiss of peace. It is an act of honesty and courage . . . of entrusting oneself, beyond sin, to the mercy that forgives . . . Thus we understand why the *confession of sins* must ordinarily be individual and not collective, just as sin is a deeply personal matter. But at the same time this confession in a way forces sin out of the secret of the heart and thus out of the area of pure individuality, emphasizing its social character as well, for through the minister of Penance it is the ecclesial community, which has been wounded by sin, that welcomes anew the repentant and forgiven sinner." (Ibid.)

Confessional: Blessed Place

Having discussed the nature of contrition in the Sacrament of Penance, Pope John Paul, in his great Apostolic Exhortation *Reconciliatio et Paenitentia*, continues with an explanation of absolution and the penitent's willingness to render satisfaction for sin.

Sacramental absolution — the words of the priest, "I absolve you . . ." and the gestures that accompany it — the symbolic imposition of the hand and the sign of the cross over the penitent — indicate that *at this moment* the contrite sinner comes into contact with God's ineffable power and mercy.

GOD, of course, is always the one, the only one, who forgives. The priest is the *minister* of divine pardon. Hence the absolution which the priest imparts in the confessional is "the effective sign of the intervention of the Father in every absolution and the sign of the 'resurrection' from 'spiritual death' which is renewed each time that the Sacrament of Penance is administered.

EXPERIENCING absolution requires faith. For "only faith can give us certainty that *at that moment* every sin is forgiven and blotted out by the mysterious intervention of the Savior."

AS FOR penitential satisfaction, it is the final act, which "crowns the sacramental sign of Penance." In some countries, the Holy Father notes, the act by which the penitent, forgiven and absolved, consents to perform after receiving absolution, is described precisely as "the *penance.*" What is the significance of this *satisfaction*?

FOR ONE thing, satisfaction is certainly "not a price that one pays for the sin absolved and for the forgiveness obtained; no human price can match what is obtained, which is the fruit of Christ's Precious Blood." No; acts of satisfaction — doing one's penance — should, while remaining simple and humble, to express more clearly all that they signify — mean several valuable things.

FIRST, writes John Paul, they constitute signs of the personal commitment that the Christian has made to God, in the Sacrament of Penance, to start a new life.

SECONDLY, these acts of satisfaction "include the idea that the pardoned sinner is able to join his own physical and spiritual mortification — which has been sought after or at least accepted — to the Passion of Jesus who has obtained the forgiveness for him."

TOO, the so-called "penance" assigned by the confessor can remind us "that even after absolution there remains . . . a dark area, due to the wound of sin, to the imperfection of love in repentance, to the weakening of the spiritual faculties. It is an area in which there still operates an infectious source of sin which must always be fought with mortification and penance."

HERE the Holy Father adds brief references to other "convictions of faith" regarding Penance.

ONE IS that "nothing is more personal and intimate than" confession. This is so because the sinner stands alone before God with his sin and repentance, and "no one can repent in his place or ask forgiveness in his name." Moreover, in sacramental penance, "everything takes place between the individual alone and God." This is not, of course, to deny the social aspect of confession, since sin affects the entire ecclesial community and since the priest, by virtue of his office, functions as the witness and representative of the ecclesial nature of Penance.

ANOTHER "conviction of faith" accented by the Holy Father is that the most precious effect of Penance consists in reconciliation with God. But this reconciliation with God "leads . . . to other reconciliations, which repair the breaches caused by sin." Thus, the penitent not only regains his own true identity (being reconciled with himself), but also is reconciled with his brethren.

CONSEQUENTLY, John Paul declares: "Every confessional is a special and blessed place from which, with divisions wiped away, there is born anew an uncontaminated, a reconciled individual — a reconciled world!"

Three Forms for Reconciliation

Among the closing paragraphs of his monumental post-Synodal Apostolic Exhortation, *Reconciliatio et Paenitentia* (2 December), Pope John Paul II discusses the three "forms of celebration" of the Sacrament of Penance.

The first is the familiar one; namely, individual confession and absolution. This, the Holy Father stresses, is "the only normal and ordinary way of celebrating the Sacrament, and it cannot and must not be allowed to fall into disuse or to be neglected."

INDIVIDUAL confession serves to highlight the *more personal, and essential*, aspects of the penitential process. Thus, the dialogue between the penitent and confessor, the choice of Scripture texts made, the "satisfaction" or "penance" assigned, all focus on the personal dimension. Moreover, this form allows for the spiritual direction of the penitent.

THE SECOND form, the reconciliation of several penitents with individual confession and absolution, accents the communal nature of sin and forgiveness. John Paul grants that this form can be "particularly meaningful at various seasons of the liturgical year and in connection with events of special pastoral importance."

ONE doctrinal point that needs stressing in the liturgy of the word preceding such communal penitential celebrations is that the Church encourages as especially useful the confession of venial sins, even though such lesser sins can be pardoned by other means; e.g., acts of sorrow, works of charity, prayer, penitential rites.

ANOTHER doctrinal point suitable for emphasis in communal services is frequent confession. The Church has always taught, and continues to teach, that frequent confession (to which priests and religious are held) is both useful and maturing. Its celebration "becomes for the faithful 'the occasion and the incentive to conform . . .' more closely to Christ and to make themselves more docile to the voice of the spirit." Besides, the grace proper to Penance "has a great remedial power and helps to remove the very roots of sin."

THE THIRD form of Penance is communal celebration with general absolution. This form, John Paul reasserts, "*cannot become an ordinary one.*" Moreover, it must not be used, save "in cases of grave necessity." Further, even when general absolution takes place according to law, "there remains unchanged the obligation to make an individual confession of serious sins before having recourse to another general absolution."

THE Holy Father's own words require repeating:

"IT IS opportune to reflect more deeply on the reasons which order the celebration of Penance in one of the first two forms and permit the use of the third form. First of all, there is the reason of *fidelity* to the will of the Lord Jesus . . . the individual integral confession of sins with individual absolution constitutes the *only ordinary way* in which the faithful who are conscious of serious sin are reconciled with God and with the Church. From this confirmation of the Church's teaching it is clear that *every serious sin must always be stated*, with its determining circumstances, *in an individual confession.*

"THEN there is a reason of the pastoral order. While it is true that, when the conditions required by canonical discipline occur, use may be made of the third form of celebration, it must not be forgotten that *this form cannot become an ordinary one*, and it cannot and must not be used — as the Synod repeated — except 'in cases of grave necessity.' And there remains unchanged the obligation to make an individual confession of serious sins before again having recourse to another general absolution. The bishop therefore, who is the only one competent in his own diocese to assess whether the conditions actually exist which Canon Law lays down for the use of the third form, will give this judgment *with a grave obligation on his own conscience*, with full respect for the law and practice of the Church, and also taking into account the criteria and guidelines agreed upon — on the basis of the doctrinal and pastoral considerations explained above — with the other members of the Episcopal Conference . . . The exceptional use of the third form of celebration must never lead to a lesser regard for, still less an abandonment of, the ordinary forms, nor must it lead to this form being considered an alternative to the other two forms.

". . . I WISH to instil into everyone the lively sense of responsibility which must guide us when we deal with sacred things like the Sacraments, which are not our property, or like consciences, which have a right not to be left in uncertainty and confusion. The Sacraments and consciences . . . are sacred, and both require that we serve them in truth."

PART TWO

A Brief Catechesis On The New Rite of Penance and The Revised Canon Law on The Sacrament of Penance

The New Rite of Penance Reviewed (1)

Q. Please review for me the new rite of confession. First, when did it become effective?

A. The new *Rite of Penance* was approved and ordered published in the Latin on 2 December 1973.

The revision was mandated by Vatican II's Constitution on the Sacred Liturgy, in this brief sentence: "The rite and formulas for the sacrament of penance are to be revised so that they more clearly express both the nature and effect of the sacrament. The first study session following the Council occurred in December 1966.

Implementation of the new rite in the English (or any vernacular) was carried out by the various national conferences of bishops.

NEW NAME

Q. Is it true that the sacrament of penance should no longer be called confession?

A. Confession is one of the three acts of the penitent in the rite of penance. (Contrition and satisfaction are the others.) For several reasons, much too complicated to analyze here, the sacrament has long been popularly called "confession," especially since the 11th century.

Traditionally, the formal name for the sacrament is the Sacrament of Penance. One problem with this phrase in our times is that the word "penance" popularly signifies the assumption of a work of mortification or expiation.

A somewhat more precise phrase, better expressive of the entire essential content of the sacrament, is the suggested traditional alternate, "Sacrament of Reconciliation."

"Reconciliation" is a traditional term, found in the Bible to designate fraternal forgiveness (Matthew 5:23-24), God's work of reuniting men among themselves (Ephesians 2:14-16) and with him (Colossians 1:20, Romans 5:10) through Jesus' cross and Resurrection. Surely one of the best known pertinent Scriptural texts is Second Corinthians 5:18-20:

"It was God who *reconciled* us to himself through Christ and gave us the work of handing on this *reconciliation*. In other words, God in Christ was reconciling the world to himself, not holding men's faults against them, and he has entrusted to us the news that they are *reconciled*. So we are ambassadors for Christ; it is as though God were appealing through us, and the appeal that we make in Christ's name is: be *reconciled* to God." (Italics added)

In the ancient Roman liturgy, the ending of this text was used in the formula for absolution.

Whereas "penance" seems, in modern language, to emphasize man's activity, "reconciliation" accents God's action in bringing men both together and Godward. Too, "reconciliation" appears better to allow for the concept of "encounter," so crucial to an understanding of sacramental mystery; in every sacrament God encounters the recipient through Christ who acts in his Church; and the recipient, a member of Christ's Church, meets the living Lord in faith.

Hence while "Sacrament of Penance" may still be used, "Sacrament of Reconciliation" is now restored to official use as an alternate descriptive. Catechetically, the restoration might stress more meaningfully the positive effect of the sacrament.

CONFESSIONAL
Q. Does the new confessional rite abolish confessionals?

A. No. The new Rite of Penance does not specifically prescribe the place where the sacrament is to be celebrated, but it leaves determination of guidelines in this area to the national conferences of bishops and individual bishops in accordance with various religious traditions and cultures.

Directive Number 12 in the new rite reads simply: "The Sacrament of Penance is celebrated in the place and location prescribed by law." And Directive Number 38b reminds the bishops of their responsibility "to determine more precise regulations about the place proper for the ordinary celebration of the sacrament . . ."

Quick View of Penance Rites (2)

Q. Could you describe in brief the new rite for confession?

A. The new Rite of Penance or Reconciliation (both phrases are traditional and acceptable) consists of three distinct ceremonies: (1) the Rite for Reconciliation of Individual Penitents, (2) the Rite for Reconciliation of Several Penitents with Individual Confession and Absolution, and (3) the Rite for Reconciliation of Several Penitents with General Confession and Absolution.

The first corresponds to what is now familiarly called "confession." The penitent blesses himself, and is invited by the priest to trust in God. (Several Scriptural invitations are given, such as "May the Lord Jesus welcome you. He came to call sinners, not the just. Have confidence in him.") Next the priest may read or recite a Bible text stressing God's mercy and his call to conversion. (Example: Mark 1:14-15)

The actual confession follows, prefaced by the Confiteor or some similar formula, according to custom. And following the confession, the act of contrition. (Several forms, all either biblically phrased or founded, are suggested. Examples: Luke 15:18, 18:13; Psalm 25:6-7.) One may of course use any traditional, approved form of expressing contrition, in whatever language he finds comfortable.

Finally, as usual, the absolution is given. The priest extends his hands, or at least his right hand, toward the penitent's head as he says the form which ends as always,

"I absolve you from your sins in the name of the Father, and of the Son and of the Holy Spirit."

The penitent responds with "Amen."

After the absolution there is a brief dismissal.

FOR GROUPS: II

THE SECOND FORM of celebrating Penance is intended for the reconciliation of a group, with provision for individual confessions. It is really a liturgical service.

It opens with an entrance psalm or hymn, after which the priest or another minister briefly explains its significance. Then the priest invites all to pray. Silence is followed by an oration. (Example: "Lord, turn to us in mercy and forgive us all our sins, that we may serve you in true freedom . . .")

Appropriate Bible readings follow. Examples: Isaiah 1:10-18; Ephesians 4:23-32; Matthew 5:1-12. Next comes the homily, which proceeds from the Bible lessons and orients toward examination of conscience and renewal.

Time for examination of conscience is then set aside; a deacon or other minister invites all to bow or kneel and join in a Confiteor. The examination of conscience closes with a litany or hymn and the Lord's Prayer. (A series of meaningful options is given in the ritual.)

Individual confession and absolution then take place.

Finally, there is a proclamation of praise for God's mercy, a solemn blessing, and the dismissal.

This second ceremony is essentially the same as that

which was in use in many parishes since Vatican II; hence it is not something entirely new, but rather represents a relatively fixed formula for such a ceremony.

GENERAL: III

THE THIRD CEREMONY is like the second, though with this major exception: it allows for a general confession and general absolution in place of individual confession and absolution — with the key provision of course that all serious sins must be confessed and absolved individually at some later date.

After the homily, the priest reminds those in the group that they must dispose themselves properly; that each must repent and resolve to turn away from sin, to make up for scandal or harm caused, and to confess all serious sins which cannot now be confessed. Some form of satisfaction is then suggested for the benefit of all.

Then the priest or a minister invites those who wish to receive absolution to indicate this by some sign. (Example: "Will those of you who wish to receive sacramental absolution please bow your heads and acknowledge that you are sinners.") There follows a Confiteor; and, if desired, a litany or song. The Lord's Prayer comes next.

The general absolution is prefaced by three prayers, each calling for an "Amen" on the part of the group. The absolution itself also calls for a concluding "Amen."

This third form is regulated by strict liturgical and canonical norms, and its use presumes that individual confession will follow.

Anxieties Over New Penance Ritual (3)

Q. Does the new Rite of Penance mandate a face-to-face confession? Or is there an option? Does it discourage frequent confession?

A. Face-to-face confession is an option; the right to a penitent's anonymity is preserved and respected.

Psychologically, anonymity is important; the humiliation which confession necessarily entails can be intensified without it. Pope Paul VI stressed this point shortly after the new rite was announced. Humanly speaking, it is not an easy thing to acknowledge and specify serious sin, which obviously evidences moral failure. Even the most enthusiastic view of Penance as a celebration cannot change this dimension of the sacrament, which is intrinsic to its valid reception.

FREEDOM

IN EVERY case the freedom of the penitent to confess in the usual way — anonymously — is safeguarded. But the option is provided for those who might wish, for their own spiritual welfare, to make their confession face to face.

To facilitate this option, so-called "confessional rooms" have been set aside in churches: rooms which can be utilized as traditional confessionals or, in accordance with Church legislation, fitting sacramental settings for face-to-face confession. However, it belongs to bishops' conferences to determine precise regulations about the place for ordinary celebration of the Sacrament of Penance.

FREQUENCY
FREQUENT confession? The Sacrament of Reconciliation assures divine forgiveness and healing: pardon and peace. Surely the traditional doctrine of frequent confession cannot be altered.

The Church has clearly addressed itself to this question in recent years. Consider this statement, for example, from the Vatican's Pastoral Norms Concerning the Administration of General Sacramental Absolution:

"Priests should be careful not to discourage the faithful from frequent or devotional confession. On the contrary, let them draw attention to its fruitfulness for Christian living ... It must be absolutely prevented that individual confession should be reserved for serious sins only ..." (Section 12)

VALUE
THESE PHRASES reflect the words of the Second Vatican Council's Decree on the Bishops' Pastoral Office in the Church; namely, "Pastors should also be mindful of how much the Sacrament of Penance contributes to developing the Christian life and, therefore, should make themselves available to hear the confessions of the faithful ..." (Section 30)

TRENT
THE CHURCH'S traditional doctrine encouraging frequent recourse to sacramental confession (once a month, say) is based on the Apostolic datum, solemnly witnessed to by the Council of Trent, that confession of sin in the Sacrament of Penance constitutes a positive value conducive to the nourishment and growth of God-life in the penitent.

This means that even though a person is not conscious of having committed a serious sin, and hence is not strictly bound to confess, his approaching the Sacrament of Penance can be a useful and spiritually advantageous act.

The reasons for this are several. One is that sacramental confession amounts to a free, external, loving, and humble surrender of a person to God in the order of forgiveness — God before whose sanctity man is graced even when obtaining pardon for the least venial fault. Hence it helps man progress Godward.

ECCLESIAL

SECONDLY, confession always represents an affirmation of the visible Church. Every sin — even a "mere" venial fault, again — insults the Body of Christ, which is the Church. Hence reparation for such injustice is most meaningfully and dramatically fulfilled if the fault is confessed to a priest, who acts as a representative and focal point of the Church. Vatican II strongly emphasizes this aspect. (Read the Dogmatic Constitution on the Church, Section II.) And the new Rite of Penance focuses on this principle strongly.

(There are of course secondary or peripheral benefits to frequent confession, such as spiritual direction. These can also be stressed, but do not really go to the heart of the matter.)

The foregoing principles relating to the importance of frequent or devotional confession are meaningful only insofar as the practice is understood and appreciated by the individual Christian. The frequency of one's confession will reflect his overall faith-commitment, his observance of the Church's liturgical year, and his own spiritual life.

Why Individual Absolution Is Norm (4)

Q. With general absolution now allowed by the Church — so I read, at least — isn't it likely that the custom of confessing our sins is rapidly on the way out, and that it's only a matter of time but that confession will be phased out altogether?

A. The Church's doctrine regarding confession is clear: the contrite confession of all mortal sins committed after baptism is required, in accordance with God's plan for forgiveness. The rumor that the Church might one day abolish confession is totally without substance.

The truth is that the Church cannot eliminate the need for confession because confession was revealed as a positive value. The Church's solemn witness to this truth occurred at the Ecumenical Council of Trent.

ONLY NORM

THE ORTHODOX doctrine is clearly reflected in the new Rite of Penance or Reconciliation:

"Individually, integral confession and absolution remain the only ordinary way for the faithful to reconcile themselves with God and the Church, unless physical or moral impossibility excuses from this kind of confession." (Number 31)

And: "Those who receive pardon for grave sins by a common absolution should go to individual confession before they receive this kind of absolution again, unless they are impeded by a just reason. They are strictly bound, unless this is morally impossible, to go to confession within a year . . ." (Number 34)

Too, in the very ceremony of general absolution, the priest must explain to those about to be absolved of the need "to confess individually at the proper time each of the serious sins which cannot then be confessed."

NOT NEW

IT IS IMPORTANT to note here that general absolution is not a modern invention of some liturgists or theologians. General absolution has always been a possibility for those who, because of grave excusing circumstances, could not confess at the time — troops about to enter combat, for example, or crowds caught in a disaster, such as an earthquake. But it has always been stressed that those so absolved and who survive the crisis must confess all serious matter.

Number 31 in the new Rite states that particular, occasional circumstances may make it lawful and even necessary to impart general absolution to a number of penitents without their already having confessed serious matters.

GRAVE NEED

GRAVE NEED is generically cited as fulfilling such circumstances, "namely, when, in view of the number of penitents, sufficient confessors are not available to hear individual confessions properly within a suitable period of time, so that the penitents would, through no fault of their own, have to go without sacramental grace or holy communion for a long time. This may happen especially in mission territories but in other places as well and also in groups of persons when the need is established." (Number 31)

Such grave need would not be verified when confessors are available, for the sole reason of a large number of penitents, e.g., during pilgrimages.

BISHOP JUDGE

WHO IS the judge of grave need as regards general absolution? The decision is left to the bishop of the diocese, who is to consult with the other members of the episcopal conference. The new Code of Canon Law regulates this precisely.

Again, those who receive general absolution are *still bound to the norm of confessing, with respect to all grave matter.* Moreover, they must be disposed by contrition, and have the intention of repairing any harm or scandal their sins may have caused, and, of course, be willing to make satisfaction for their guilt.

Two 'Now' Errors Pertaining To Penance (5)

Q. Two questions regarding the new Rite of Penance occur to me. The first has to do with the trend today to view the priest in the confessional as a psychological counselor. Is it remotely possible that the new rite deliberately caters to this view, in the sense that it encourages a confessional room, rather than the traditional confessional?

A. No, it is not even remotely possible that the new Rite of Penance somehow serves the theory — the erroneous theory, of course — that the minister of the sacrament functions essentially in the manner of a psychological counselor.

The confessional and the psychologist's (or psychiatrist's) office are two distinct entities. The first is sacramental; the latter, scientific. Each has a different primary purpose: the confessional relates directly to real guilt, guilt for sin; psychology relates to neurotic or emotional guilt.

REAL GUILT
IN THE SACRAMENT of penance, the priest absolves from real guilt. Real guilt results from the commission of sin, which constitutes a deliberate offense against God. When sin is contritely confessed and the intention to satisfy for it is offered, the guilt is taken away forever through the mystery of Christ's redeeming death and Resurrection, by virtue of the power of the keys of heaven, which the priest enjoys.

Neurotic or emotional guilt is either imaginary guilt or that guilt feeling which can remain after real guilt is absolved from. (Sin adversely affects the total person, hence, his emotions.) Sometimes this guilt can be irrationally exaggerated, or else distorted out of perspective. Sometimes, too, it cannot be readily handled because of a host of complex personal problems.

A confessor must be spiritually sensitive to penitents who have difficulties with emotional guilt, of course. He must be able to recognize guilt feelings, isolate them, and, if necessary, refer those troubled by such guilt to professional psychological or psychiatric help.

"The priest," explains Dr. John R. Cavanagh, "in restoring spiritual health, may also, in a secondary or accidental manner assist in restoring bodily or mental well-being. This, however, is not his principal purpose. The soul in the state of sin is not necessarily mentally ill. Confession is not a substitute for psychotherapy; neurotic guilt is not real guilt . . . The psychiatrist . . . is concerned only with feelings of guilt which are delusional and distorted and not based on objective reality . . ." (*Pastoral Counseling*; Bruce, 1962)

Priestly ministry in confession cannot be reduced to psychological counseling. In fact, both areas are distinct, though both may accidentally overlap. Confession has to do with sin and real guilt; and this real guilt is take away forever by priestly absolution. Psychological counseling cannot take away real guilt.

NOT MERE DIALOGUE
Q. Is it possible that the New Rite of Penance redefines the sacrament primarily in terms of a "dialogue of reconciliation" between minister and penitent, and that

the priest's absolution is only a prayer that God will impart pardon to the penitent? I get the impression that some religious education teachers are now teaching this. True or not?

A. To view the sacrament of penance primarily, or simply, in terms of a dialogue, followed by a ministerial prayer for pardon, is clearly in error.

Dialogue can and should ordinarily take place within the rite of the sacrament, of course. The new ritual urges conversation between minister and penitent.

But it is of faith that the priest-confessor functions as a judge as well as a healer, counselor and father; this doctrine was solemnly reaffirmed by a definition during the Council of Trent.

Sacramental absolution therefore constitutes a judicial action, for which there is required the presentation of a "case," known as confession. This follows from Jesus' own will in instituting the sacrament.

Absolution, moreover, is an act of Holy Orders, by which the priest bestows pardon in Christ's name. It is not just a petition that God may forgive, but an actual proclamation that God forgives.

Note that the priest does not say, "I pray that God may absolve you"; but rather, "I absolve you . . ." The grammatical form is not petitionary, but indicative; the tense of the verb is not future, but present tense indicative.

Absolution is not simply a wish, but a fact; a declaration of grace, not a hope; a statement, not a promise.

The New Code on Sacrament of Penance (6)

Q. Does the new Code of Canon Law change anything regarding confession? Does it reiterate that all serious sins must be confessed? Does it allow general absolution? Does it encourage frequent confession? What about first confession?

A. The section on the Sacrament of Penance in the new *Codex Juris Canonici* (The Code of Canon Law) appears in Book IV, Title IV, Canons 959 to 991 inclusive.

Canon 959 is the "theme" canon, comparable to 870 of the 1918 Code. It explains the "right disposition" for Penance; namely, contrition and satisfaction. And it stresses that Penance not only remits sins, but reconciles the penitent with the Church — another accent on the communitarian nature of our faith.

INTEGRAL

Canon 960 reaffirms the doctrine that individual, integral confession is the ordinary means by which the faithful who are conscious of grave sin are reconciled with God and the Church; that, moreover, only physical or moral impossibility excuses from confession.

Canon 988, Paragraph 1 — I'm citing the canons out of sequence here — reminds that Christians are obliged to confess, according to species and number, all serious postbaptismal sins not yet directly submitted to the power of the Church's keys — not yet confessed in an individual confession — following a diligent examination of conscience. Paragraph 2 of this canon commends the confession of venial sins as well.

Canon 989 requires, after the age of discretion, at least an annual faithful confession of grave sins.

Canon 961 — now I'm backtracking — begins with the norm that general absolution (absolution given to many at the same time without individual confession on the part of each involved) ordinarily cannot be given, unless: (1) there is danger of death and not time for a priest or priests to hear the confessions of all (Paragraph 1); (2) there is grave need, as when, in view of the number of penitents, sufficient priests are not available to hear individual confessions properly within a suitable period of time, so that the penitents would, through no fault of their own, have to go without sacramental grace or Holy Communion for a long time.

General absolution is not lawful — need is not justified, in other words — when confessors are not available merely for the sole reason of the large number of penitents, as can happen on the occasion of a major liturgical feast or pilgrimage. (These norms reflect those already contained in the *Rite of Penance*, Introduction, No. 31.)

Paragraph 3 states that the judgment regarding the above conditions and the determination regarding the lawfulness of conferring general absolution are reserved to the bishop of the diocese, who is to consult with the other members of the conference of bishops.

Canon 962 declares that anyone who receives general absolution should resolve to confess individually in due time any grave sins which he is unable to confess at present; it is also necessary, of course, that a penitent be rightly disposed (i.e., contrite and willing to make satisfaction).

Canon 963 adds that the recipient of general absolution is bound to submit, in an individual confession, all grave matter thus absolved, *quam primum, occasione data* ("as soon as possible, the opportunity given" is the way I translate this) before he receives general absolution again, unless he is impeded by a just reason.

FIRST CONFESSION

The Canon referring to first confession prior to first Communion appears under the title of the Blessed Eucharist; there Canon 914 reminds parents and pastors to prepare children for first Communion when they reach the age of discretion, *praemissa sacramentali confessione* ("sacramental confession having already occurred" — translation mine).

Canon 965 restates that the minister of the Sacrament of Penance is only a priest or bishop (*solus sacerdos*). To facilitate the availability of Penance, priests are authorized to hear confessions anywhere, as long as they have faculties from their own bishops.

Canon 964 has to do with the proper place of confession; i.e., a church or oratory. It also describes the confessional, and requires that the option of anonymity be secured by a fixed grille.

Some Closing Thoughts

One of the two principal themes of the Blessed Virgin Mary's appearances at Lourdes in France was conversion from sin. Pope John Paul II strongly accented this theme during his pilgrimage to the Shrine there in mid-August, 1983.

Preaching in the Lourdes Grotto on Sunday afternoon, 14 August, the Holy Father explained that conversion and penance sound strange to a world which has lost its concept of sin:

"TODAY, even the sense of sin has partly disappeared, because the meaning of God is being lost. Some have thought of evolving a humanism without God, and the faith might easily be seen as something peculiar to a few, without its necessary role for the salvation of all. Consciences have become dulled, as on the occasion of the first sin, no longer able to distinguish between good and evil. Many no longer know what sin is, or do not want to know, as if this knowledge would destroy their freedom . . .

"THE VIRGIN without sin reminds us . . . She tells us, as she told Bernadette: pray for sinners, come wash yourselves, purify yourselves . . ."

RECONCILIATION and penance were also the main subjects of the Pope's sermon during Lauds at the Basilica of the Rosary on Monday, 15 August, the second day of his pilgrimage to Lourdes. Speaking to 500 priest confessors and other religious, he said:

"WE ARE obviously puzzled by the large number of

faithful who abandon this sacrament of Penance while only a few turn to it or even return to it in a fruitful way. We will do everything to instruct and convince the faithful of the need to receive forgiveness in a personal, fervent and frequent manner. And we will take great care to exercise this ministry as the Church wants us to, so that no one will abandon it on the pretext that he finds the celebration of this sacrament formal or superficial . . ."

EARLIER, in the same homily, Pope John Paul prayed:

"O CHRIST, revive in us and in all the priests of the world this truly paschal gift! This gift destined to make humanity, always inclined to sin, pass from death to life! On that Easter evening, you could already see, Lord, the use we would make of this gift which sprang from your heart, as did the other sacraments. You knew the hours of toil and joy that we would devote to this ministry, so sublime and yet so human. There exist today trends of thought which minimize the notion of sin and by the same token, depreciate the power of forgiveness given in ordination . . ."

HERE I detect another dimension of today's problem of dwindling confessional lines; namely, the dwindling number of priests. It is almost as if the Holy Father were saying — actually he comes quite close to affirming it — that priestly vocations are waning largely because the sense of sin is waning in the world. What need is there for priests if there is no sin — no personal sin — in the world? If sin does not exist, there is no need for forgiveness, hence no need for sacramental confession, consequently no need for priests, who say, *"I absolve you . . ."* In this context, is there any need for Redemption?

AGAIN it must be admitted that John Paul II is a Pope whose mind penetrates into the essence of problems — not without prophetic vision, of course. A people who claims themselves sinless, and therefore in no need of sacramental confession (and, for that reason, in no need of priest confessors) constitutes a generation that in effect claims itself independent of Christ the Savior. *Sinless, why require salvation?*